NEWS RELEASE TRADING

LEARN HOW TO TRADE THE NEWS AS A BUSINESS | ONLINE BUSINESS TRADING STRATEGIES | Pandemic BUSINESS | FX TRADING

PAUL ARDENNES

I0504933

This book was published thanks to free support and training from:

The Wall Street Investors' Club

Table of Contents

CHAPTER 1. MAP OF COURSE

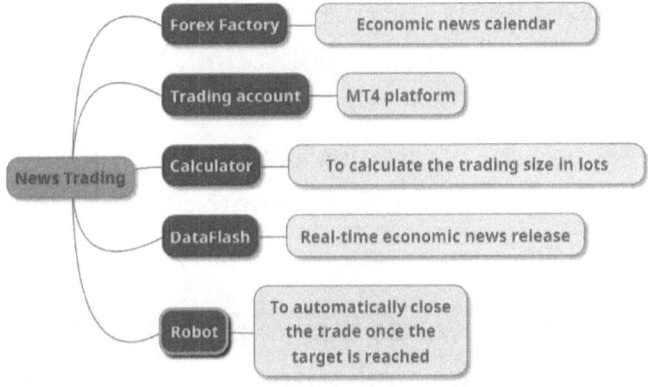

Chapter 2. Introduction

The online application

In order to know the direction to trade, we use a small online real time application. It is available on the website https:wallstreetinvestors.club under the tab "Strategies" and "News". It is free for 14 days and then $10/month at time of writing this.

If the news are worse than expected in the forecast, then the application will show a red band on the left of the centerline. This indicates that the trade is a "Sell" for the base currency.

As an example, if the currency in the News is the USD, and you choose the USDJPY as your trading chart, then a red band would indicate a sell for the USDJPY. If on the other hand, you choose the EURUSD, the EUR being the base currency, i.e. the first one, the one in front, then you would "Buy" the EURUSD; that means that you are actually selling the USD. It is easy to get this wrong, so please make sure you do understand it. You would be trading the wrong way otherwise. The way I overcome the problem is by only using charts where the base currency is the one in the News. Like this I never get it wrong.

If the news are much better than expected in the forecast, the application will show a blue band on the right of the centerline. This indicates that the trade is a "Buy" for the base currency. The base currency is the one that comes first in the pair, the one in front. If the news are for the USD and your chart is on the EURUSD, then a blue band on the USD news would indicate that you "Sell" the EUR, which is the same thing as buying the USD. Get this right or your trading will be wrong.

We don't trade if the news are neutral or less than ¾ the band size. Please note that your order may not be filled first time. You may need to continue pressing the order button (Buy or Sell) until the order is placed. I suggest that if this happens, *you wait for a little retracement to half way the spike* so that you get the order at a better price. If this does not happen, don't trade. That way, you lose nothing.

Write your notes here....

Notes writing here....

ECONOMIC NEWS CALENDAR

Before starting the day, we check on [Forex Factory website](#) whether there are any news this day. This is simply to know what currency to trade and the time the news are released. We can then calculate our number of lots to trade and set up our exit robot. You will need to make sure that the time is correctly set up on the calendar website. Then you will need to filter the news so that you only get the "High Impact" News, the red ones. We only trade the High Impact News in this course as the volatility is good enough. It's explained in one of the videos in the course.

Write your notes here....

CALCULATOR

To know precisely our level of risk, we use a trading calculator that is available on the website under the tab "Trading Calculator"

There is a training video to teach how to use it for the particular course that you are studying.

If you are a funded trader, then you need to comply with the maximum number of lots indicated by the funders. There is a small calculator for this purpose.

Capital	87500		
Total # of trades	5	Total allowance	4.375
Maximum lots per trade	0.875		

The rule of thumb is that we can trade 0.5 lots maximum per $10K capital. We input the capital available and the number of trades that we plan to have on the day. The calculator will tell us the maximum number of lots for each open order.

usdjpy

		USD	EUR	GBP
Stop Loss	50			
Take Profit	50			
Capital		10000	40000	40000
Risk %		2.000%	0.250%	0.250%
Money risked		200	100	100
Profit expected		200	100	100
# of Lots		*0.426*	*0.237*	*0.259*
		5 Digit	3 Digit	2 Digit
Entry Price		1.75390	145.342	1230.59
Direction (B/S)		S	S	S
SL		1.75890	145.842	1235.59
TP		1.74890	144.842	1225.59

Notes taking....

Write your notes here....

TRADING ACCOUNT

We use the MT4 platform for placing orders with our funding institutions. If you use a broker, you may use any platform but this course uses MT4. There is a strategy tester that we use from time to time. The minimum that is tradable in term of capital is $50. This is because the MT4 platform has a minimum of 0.01 lot risk parameter. A funded account will have the mention "live" on MT4. A non-funded account will have either "Live" or "Demo" depending on your own choice of trading. We suggest that you use a demo account of $10000 to duplicate our funded trading. We try to show our demo accounts setup whenever possible on our website. If one day, the investors allow us to show live accounts, these will be introduced on the website.

Write your notes here...

Exit robot

Because the Economic News Release is a high volatility event, it happens quickly, we use an exit robot to close the trade. Sometimes, we can be in and out of a trade in a few seconds. To enable a speedy and organized exit, we use a robot that you can download from here. It is called "Close all at equity level" if you need to google it one day. See the clickable image below to access it direct.

CloseAllAtEquityLevel.mq4   5 KB | 3,114 downloads
CloseAllAtEquityLevel.ex4   5 KB | 1,513 download

CHAPTER 4. INTERMEZZO

In the set of videos in the course, you will arrange the business in such a way that you trade the news **real time** as soon as they appear. We tried to find a free real time news application but did not manage.

OUTLINE OF THE TRADING SETUP

1   - First we check the news on the calendar. We keep note of the time and currency.

2   - We set up a chart of that currency. If the News is on the USD, we normally use the USDJPY since the USD and the JPY sessions are not connected. For the EUR, we would normally use the EURJPY and for the GBP we would choose the GBPJPY. You can experiment to see what ones react most with news. If fact, we could set up different charts to see where the biggest spike happens.

3   - We check the capital available and determine the exit level. We aim at 2.5% gain/loss with an overall 10% monthly gain. For those who are just starting, a reasonable gain/loss % would be 0.5%. We would input

this in the calculator to get a lot value. We place the exit robot on the chart before the trading starts.

4   - We calculate the number of lots that we will be using for this trade. We select the currency on the calculator, input the capital available and the risk that we wish to take. We copy the number of lots to our trading platform in the order window, making sure that we have selected the correct currency pair.

5   - We set up the chart on M1, shifted left and magnified to its biggest size minus one (we press the + button until we can't anymore and then press once the – button) It makes things clearer to see and appreciate the size of the spike that is created as a result of the News release.

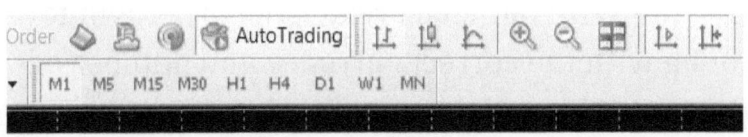

6   - We open the news application from the website and get ready for the announcement to occur. The speaker will announce "One minute before release" and then "10 seconds before release".

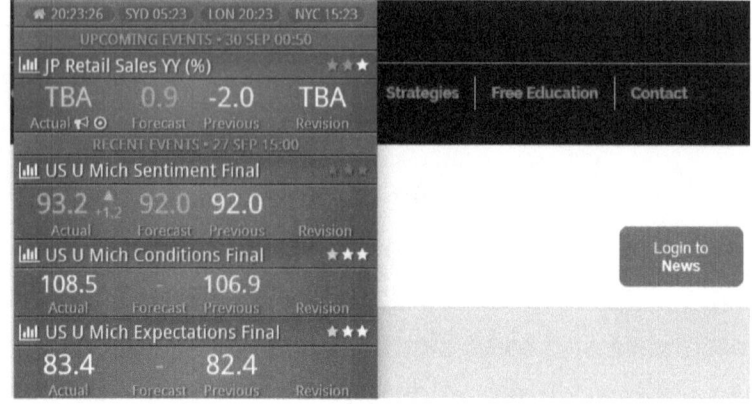

We need to be on the active trader tab to trade the news.

7 – With our chart ready, the order window open with the correct currency and number of lots, and the real time application ready, we wait until the announcement is finished. Bands will happen on the real time application, either red or blue or Red and Blue if several High Impact News are released at the same time. We don't trade these unless they are all in the same color.

The videos in the course show the perfect trading setup

And that is pretty much it. Try it, test it and be patient but be quick.

Happy Pips.

About The Author

Paul Ardennes

Researcher in Energy fields, programmer and forex scientist

"Paul Ardennes is an Author. He is working with various publishers including *Amazon* and *Barnes & Noble*.

He publishes courses on educational platforms such as *Udemy* & *Simpliv on Spiritual Yoga and Forex trading*.

He is a trained Electronic Medicine practitioner (Scenar Cosmodic, Auricular therapy, Acupoints charting, electronic iris analysis, laser therapy and so on...), **an energy healer** (Seichim and Usui Reiki Master, informational medicine) **and a Forex researcher** (Algorithmic trading, neural networks and artificial intelligence programming, fundamentals and technical fx trading).

He was introduced to Forex while researching yet another book. To cut a short story shorter, he got involved in forex competitions and started winning them and collecting money prizes.

That is when he discovered *Wall Street Investors' Club*, a private club where you enter by personal invitation only. They funded his trading skills.

His goal is to **impart stillness and silentness** within the emotional, turmoiled and turbulent minds of societies. He developed *Spiritual Yoga* to help with this ambition. Whether you join him to trade Forex for a second income or join him in the quest to inward peace and calm, the choice is there either way.

He is married to a Doctor gynaecologist and has 1 son. They all live in Central America.

Join the parties. Join the Clubs"

Amazon Editorial Vine Team Member

COURSES BY PAUL ARDENNES

News release trading | FX Trading | Forex | Online Business

NEW · 21 lectures · 1 hour · All Levels

Learn how to trade the news as a business | Online Business trading strategies | Use as a Hobby or business | fx trading | By **Paul Ardennes**

London Open|Trade what bankers trade every morning | Forex

NEW · 15 lectures · 38 mins · All Levels

The London Open trading system is the most popular fx trading strategy online |Unique Algorithmic trading system | | By **Paul Ardennes**

Forex Trading| Algorithmic trading | Wall Street Investors

NEW · 23 lectures · 1 hour · All Levels

FX Trading | Trading Forex with Trading Robots | The easy and smart way of trading the forex with algorithmic trading | By **Paul Ardennes**

www.ingramcontent.com/pod-product-compliance
Lightning Source LLC
Chambersburg PA
CBHW031510210526
45463CB00008B/3179